CROATIA TRAVEL GUIDE 2024

Explore the Coastline, Islands, and National Parks with what to do, see and eat

Sarah K. Cox

TABLE OF CONTENT

Chapter 1: Introduction

Croatia, located at the crossroads of Central Europe and the Mediterranean, entices visitors with an enticing blend of natural beauty, rich history, and warm hospitality. Welcome to "Croatia Unveiled," your passport to one of Europe's most alluring destinations. In the year 2024, we invite you to embark on an unforgettable journey through this captivating country, where ancient traditions meet modern wonders and every cobblestone street seems to whisper tales of ages past.

You are not just holding a book in your hands; you are seizing the opportunity to unearth the treasures of a long-hidden nation. Croatia is a land where emerald green forests meet the Sapphire Adriatic Sea, medieval towns blend seamlessly with modern cities, and cuisine is a sensory experience. This guide has been meticulously crafted to satisfy your every desire, whether you are an adventurous explorer, a history buff, a beach lover, or a culinary connoisseur.

In "Croatia Unveiled," we want to go above and beyond the ordinary. To discover Croatia's essence, we scoured the Adriatic coast, delved deep into the heart of Istria, and ventured off the beaten path. Our vision is to be more than just another travel guide; we want to be your trusted companion, revealing the secrets and soul of this extraordinary country. This is your chance to see Croatia in 2024 like you've never seen it before.

What You Should Expect:

Explore the rugged beauty of the Dalmatian coast, wander through the lush vineyards of Istria, and immerse yourself in the captivating landscapes of Central Croatia.

The history of Croatia can be found in every stone, every church, and every festival. Our tour guide will take you on a journey through time, from Roman ruins to medieval fortresses, and into a world of vibrant traditions and events that continue to shape the country's identity.

Gastronomic Delights: Our culinary excursions will introduce you to the flavors of Croatia. We'll take your taste buds on a culinary adventure you won't soon forget, from fresh seafood from the coast to hearty continental dishes.

Outdoor Adventures: Croatia is a playground for thrill seekers. Snorkel in crystal-clear waters, hike the rugged peaks of national parks, or sail the Adriatic.

Practical Advice: We provide you with important transportation, lodging, and safety information. Say farewell to the stress of planning and hello to the freedom to fully enjoy your Croatian adventure.

With "Croatia Unveiled," we hope to pique your curiosity and inspire you to make better travel choices. More than the places you'll visit, our story is about the experiences you'll have, the stories you'll tell, and the connections you'll make. Croatia's natural beauty is well-known, but it is the untold stories, hidden gems, and genuine warmth of its people that distinguish it.

This is your invitation to go on a journey. Croatia awaits you, and the 2024 edition of "Croatia Unveiled" will help you discover its treasures. Prepare to learn about, experience, and fall in love with a country that will steal your heart at every turn. Croatia is waiting for you, and we're here to make your journey nothing short of spectacular.

Welcome to Croatia

Croatia is a land of timeless beauty and stories. When you step onto its picturesque shores, you are not just entering a country; you are embarking on a journey through history, culture, and the breathtaking landscapes that have captured the hearts of travelers for generations.

Croatia's Welcome Mat: All visitors to its shores are greeted with a genuine and warm welcome. The phrase "Pomalo," which means "take it easy," encapsulates Croatian hospitality and reflects the country's relaxed and welcoming atmosphere. Whether you're wandering the historic streets of Dubrovnik, sipping coffee in Zagreb's cafes, or relaxing on an island hideaway, you'll be greeted with smiles and open arms the moment you step foot in Croatia.

A Tapestry of Landscapes: Croatia's geography is a tapestry of diverse landscapes. From the rugged Adriatic coast with its jewel-like islands to the rolling hills of Istria and the lush forests of Plitvice Lakes National Park, Croatia's natural beauty is breathtaking. Each region has its distinct personality, offering a wide range of experiences, whether you want to relax on sun-kissed beaches, hike in pristine national parks, or enjoy the thrill of watersports in crystal-clear waters.

Croatia's history is etched in every stone, from the Roman ruins of Pula to the medieval walls of Dubrovnik and the architectural wonders of Split. Echoes of centuries past can be heard all over the country. As you walk through the streets of Diocletian's Palace, you will come across ancient amphitheaters and centuries-old monasteries. Every corner of Croatia has a story to tell, and your journey will allow you to add your chapter to its illustrious history.

Cultural Harmony: Croatia's cultural heritage is a vibrant mosaic of influences. Its traditions, customs, and festivals are a mash-up of Roman, Venetian, Ottoman, and Austro-Hungarian legacies. Local celebrations, traditional music, and the intricate craftsmanship displayed in artisanal products all contribute to this colorful tapestry. Don't miss the vibrant folk festivals and klapa harmonies that define Croatia's cultural identity.

A sensory delight: Croatian cuisine is a culinary paradise. Croatian cuisine demonstrates the country's culinary prowess, ranging from fresh seafood along the coast to hearty inland dishes. Local wines and olive oils, coastal specialties like octopus salad and black risotto, and traditional dishes like Peka and Prut are all available. Croatian cuisine is a delectable flavor exploration and celebration of local ingredients.

Your adventure begins in this land where every stone has a story to tell. Croatia's allure stems from its remarkable combination of heritage and modernity, nature and civilization, peace and adventure. So, take your time, immerse yourself in Croatia's rich tapestry of experiences, and allow the stories etched in its landscapes and the warmth of its people to enchant you. Welcome to Croatia, a country rich in adventure, history, and natural beauty.

Getting Ready for Your Trip

The prospect of visiting Croatia is thrilling in and of itself. Visitors are welcome to this land of azure seas, historic towns, and natural wonders. To ensure a smooth and rewarding adventure, it is critical to plan ahead of time. Here's how to get ready for your Croatia trip.

Travel Documents: Start with the basics. Check that your passport is valid for at least six months after the date of your intended departure. Depending on your nationality, you may need a visa to enter Croatia, so check the visa requirements ahead of time and apply if necessary. Duplicates of important travel documents, such as your passport, should also be made and kept separate from the originals.

When traveling abroad, travel insurance is your safety net. It provides you with peace of mind in the event of an unforeseeable event, such as a flight cancellation, a medical emergency, or lost luggage. Choose a policy that meets your needs and read the terms and conditions thoroughly.

When to Go: Croatia is a year-round destination with distinct charms in each season. During the summer, the Adriatic coast comes alive with beachgoers and outdoor festivals. If you prefer milder weather and fewer crowds, visit in the spring or autumn. Zagreb, in particular, has a magical atmosphere during the winter, with holiday markets and festivities.

Croatia's official currency is the Croatian Kuna (HRK). While credit cards are widely accepted, it's a good idea to keep some cash on hand for small purchases and places that don't accept cards. Currency exchange services are available at banks, ATMs, and exchange offices.

Although Croatian is the official language, English is commonly heard in tourist areas. Learning a few basic Croatian phrases will allow you to connect with locals and enhance your overall experience.

Depending on your travel plans, make sure you're up to date on routine vaccinations and consider hepatitis A and B vaccinations. Croatia is a safe country for tourists in general, but precautions should always be taken.

Maintain vigilance over your belongings, be aware of your surroundings, and follow local advice.

Pack Wisely: Bring clothing that is appropriate for the season of your visit. Summer clothing should be lightweight and breathable, whereas layers may be required in the spring and autumn. Bring comfortable walking shoes, as exploring Croatia's cobblestone streets and hiking trails is best done on foot. Please dress modestly if you intend to visit churches or historical sites.

Croatia uses 230V/50Hz European two-pin plugs. If your devices require it, bring the necessary plug adapter and voltage converter.

Itinerary: Plan your itinerary ahead of time and book your accommodations, especially during peak season. Accommodation in Croatia ranges from charming guesthouses to luxury resorts and city-center apartments. Whether you prefer to stay on the coast or immerse yourself in the history of Croatia's old towns, there is something for everyone.

Local Transportation: Learn about the various modes of transportation available in Croatia. The country has a well-developed bus system, ferries, and a growing domestic flight network. If you plan to visit less-traveled areas of the country, consider renting a car.

If you have your travel documents in order, are prepared for health and safety, and have a well-planned itinerary, you're well on your way to an unforgettable Croatian adventure. Croatia's natural beauty and cultural treasures await you, and your preparedness ensures a smooth journey from the moment you set foot on its enthralling shores. Prepare for an unforgettable adventure in a land where history, nature, and hospitality coexist harmoniously. Croatia is ready for you!

When to Visit

Choosing the best time to visit Croatia can have a big impact on your vacation. This lovely country has plenty to offer, from sun-kissed beaches to historic city centers and pristine national parks. Here's a guide to help you decide when to visit Croatia based on your preferences and interests.

Summertime (June to August):

- Summer is when Croatia comes to life, particularly along the Adriatic coast. The weather is pleasant and sunny, making it an ideal destination for beachgoers, water sports enthusiasts, and those looking for a vibrant nightlife scene.

- Festivals and Events: There are numerous festivals throughout the summer, including music and cultural events. The Dubrovnik Summer Festival is the most well-known of these, transforming the historic city into an open-air performance venue.
- Summer is the best time to visit Croatia's beautiful islands. For pristine beaches, charming towns, and a relaxed Mediterranean atmosphere, visit Hvar, Bra, or Korula.

Autumn (September through October) and Spring (April through May):

- Milder Climate: Spring and autumn offer milder weather, fewer crowds, and lower prices than the peak season. The weather is ideal for exploring historic towns and national parks, so now is an excellent time to go sightseeing.
- In Istria and Dalmatia, autumn is the harvest season for grapes and olives. Wine lovers can go on wine tours and tastings, and foodies can sample the season's culinary offerings.

Between November and March:

- While the coast is quieter in the winter, cities such as Dubrovnik and Split retain their distinct charm. Stroll through historic streets away from the crowds and enjoy coastal beauty in a tranquil setting.
- Zagreb's Winter Wonderland: The capital comes alive during the winter with festive markets, ice skating rinks, and a cozy atmosphere. While experiencing the holiday magic, sample traditional winter treats such as fritule and mulled wine.

Your interests and preferences will determine the best time to visit Croatia. Summer is the obvious choice for sun worshippers, while spring and autumn are better choices for those who prefer fewer crowds and milder temperatures. Winter, with its distinct offerings, is an excellent choice for those seeking to discover a new side of Croatia.

Chapter 2: Exploring Croatia's Regions

Istria: Located in the north, Istria is known for its rolling vineyards, ancient towns like Rovinj, and a delectable culinary scene that features truffle-infused dishes.

Dalmatia: Along the stunning Adriatic coast, Dalmatia shines with historic gems like Split and Dubrovnik. It's a beachgoer's and Mediterranean cuisine enthusiast's dream.

Explore Zagreb's cultural treasures as well as central Croatia's enchanting Plitvice Lakes, a wonderland of cascading waterfalls.

Slavonia: Croatia's eastern border enchants with untouched landscapes, wineries, and a strong folklore connection. Each region offers a distinct experience, resulting in a mosaic of Croatia's beauty and diversity.

Istria: The Northern Gem

The Istrian Peninsula in northern Croatia is a hidden treasure just waiting to be discovered. This charming region is ideal for those seeking a harmonious blend of natural beauty, historic towns, and culinary delights. The allure of Istria is found in its captivating landscapes, rich cultural heritage, and tantalizing culinary scene.

The Story of Eden:

Istria is nicknamed "Green Istria" due to its lush landscapes. Vineyards as far as the eye can see produce some of Croatia's best wines and olive oils. Hilltop towns dot the picturesque countryside, each with its distinct personality. Gronjan, Motovun, and Hum are among the most charming, offering spectacular panoramic views and a glimpse into Istria's rich history.

Cities with a History:

Every cobblestone street bears traces of Istria's past. The Pula Arena is one of the best-preserved Roman amphitheaters and a testament to Istria's ancient past. In contrast, Rovinj's romantic old town is a maze of narrow alleys, vibrant squares, and colorful facades that tumble into the Adriatic Sea. Exploring the historic towns of Istria is like stepping back in time, with each stone whispering stories from centuries gone by.

Culinary Extravaganza:

Istria is well-known for its truffles, olive oils, and wines. The cuisine of the region combines Mediterranean flavors with influences from central Europe. Istria is famous for its truffle dishes, which range from truffle-infused pasta to creamy truffle risottos. Olive oil tastings at local mills provide insight into the meticulous process of creating this liquid gold. In addition, the wine cellars are an ideal setting for sampling Istrian Malvazija and Teran.

Attractions on the Coast:

Istria's coastal towns are a haven for beachgoers and watersports enthusiasts. Pore has a lovely waterfront and crystal-clear waters ideal for swimming and snorkeling, as well as the stunning Euphrasian Basilica. The Brijuni Islands, a short boat ride from Fazana, offer pristine natural beauty, including a safari park with free-roaming animals. If you prefer more private beaches, Istria's coastline is dotted with hidden coves and bays where you can find your slice of Adriatic paradise.

Outdoor Recreation:

Istria's varied terrain makes it an ideal destination for outdoor enthusiasts. Hike, bike, or even paraglide through the rolling hills and picturesque landscapes. The Cape Kamenjak nature park is a popular destination for nature lovers due to its rugged coastline and untouched beauty.

Dalmatia: Sun, Sea, and History

Dalmatia, the crown jewel of Croatia's Adriatic coast, entices visitors with an enticing combination of natural beauty, historic riches, and endless sunshine. Dalmatia is an irresistible invitation to explore its ancient towns, soak up the Mediterranean sun, and immerse yourself in a captivating tapestry of culture and history.

Area of Recreation on the Adriatic Sea:

Dalmatia's coast is a gleaming paradise. Its crystal-clear waters, picturesque beaches, and a plethora of islands make it a beachgoer's, sailor's, and water sports enthusiast's paradise. Dalmatia's coastal beauty will captivate you whether you're relaxing on the pebble beaches of Makarska, diving into the azure depths off the island of Vis, or exploring the pristine coves of Bra.

Historic Attractions:

Dalmatia is rich in historical sites. Split, home to the UNESCO-listed Diocletian's Palace, is the city's crowning glory. This sprawling palace complex built by a Roman emperor remains the heart and soul of the city, with its labyrinthine alleys, bustling markets, and an impressive cathedral. Trogir, a nearby ancient town, has an intact medieval core that transports visitors back in time.

Dubrovnik, the Adriatic Pearl:

No trip to Dalmatia is complete without a stop in Dubrovnik, the "Pearl of the Adriatic." This historic city is surrounded by mighty walls and is a wonder of Gothic, Renaissance, and Baroque architecture. Stroll down Stradun, the city's limestone-paved main street, and visit the Rector's Palace and Maritime Museum to learn about the city's rich maritime history.

Cultural Customs:

Dalmatia is known for its diverse cultural heritage. Folk festivals and celebrations fill the streets with music and dance, and traditional klapa singing can be heard in local cafes and squares. Discover the ancient art of stone masonry, as seen in the intricate carvings on historic buildings and handed down through generations.

Delights from the Kitchen:

Dalmatian cuisine is a delectable fusion of Mediterranean flavors. The region's culinary stars are fresh seafood, olive oil, and aromatic herbs. There's black risotto, grilled fish, and anpeekak, a traditional slow-cooked meal baked under an iron bell. Pair your meals with local wines such as the renowned Plavac Mali to experience the joy of Dalmatian dining.

Outdoor Recreation:

Dalmatia's varied landscape entices outdoor enthusiasts. Hike through the rugged terrain of Biokovo Nature Park or discover the pristine lakes and waterfalls of Krka National Park. For thrill-seekers, canyoning and rafting on the Cetina River promise unforgettable experiences.

Central Croatia: Inland Wonders

While the coastal regions of Croatia are frequently the focus of attention, Central Croatia, with its rolling hills, picturesque villages, and captivating cultural heritage, has a different kind of allure. This inland region, which is frequently overlooked by visitors en route to the Adriatic, is a land of hidden treasures, historic gems, and unspoiled landscapes.

Croatia's capital, Zagreb:

Croatia's vibrant capital city, Zagreb, serves as the region's focal point. Zagreb welcomes visitors with historic architecture, lively street cafes, and a vibrant cultural scene. Explore Upper Town's medieval streets, see the iconic St. Mark's Church, and stroll through the bustling Dolac Market. Zagreb's museums, galleries, and festivals offer a taste of the city's cultural wealth.

Towns with a Baroque Heritage:

Central Croatia is home to several historic baroque towns, each with its distinct character. Because of its well-preserved architecture, Varazdin hosts one of Europe's most renowned baroque festivals. Karlovac is famous for its star-shaped fortress, and the Neanderthal Museum in Krapina tells an intriguing story of human evolution.

Nature's Peace:

The region's rolling hills, vineyards, and forests create a tranquil landscape ideal for nature lovers. Plitvice Lakes National Park, with its cascading waterfalls, crystal-clear lakes, and lush vegetation, is a UNESCO World Heritage site. Hikers and photographers will appreciate the park's enchanting combination of natural beauty.

Cultural Customs:

Central Croatia takes pride in its diverse cultural heritage. In the picturesque village of Kumrovec, visit the birthplace of Yugoslavia's former president, Josip Broz Tito. Ceramics and lacemaking are traditional crafts that are still practiced in villages such as Samobor and Akovo. The annual Akovo Horse Show, which features Lipizzaner horses, is a cultural highlight.

Delights from the Kitchen:

Central Croatia offers a one-of-a-kind culinary experience. Indulge in hearty continental dishes made with cabbage, potatoes, and freshwater fish. Try truly, a delicious pastry filled with cottage cheese, and sip local wines from the vineyards on the hillsides. Each course pays homage to the region's agricultural traditions and warm hospitality.

Healing Waters of Zagorje:

The Zagorje hills are dotted with numerous spa towns with thermal springs and wellness centers. In picturesque natural settings, Terme Tuhelj and Stubicke Toplice offer rejuvenating treatments and relaxation. Soak in thermal pools, mud baths, and saunas for a relaxing retreat.

Slavonia: The Eastern Frontier

Croatia's eastern border, Slavonia, offers a distinct and less-explored side of the country. Slavonia promises authentic experiences and a deeper connection to Croatia's roots. It is famous for its untouched landscapes, rich agricultural heritage, and cultural tapestry woven from various influences.

A Diverse Landscape: Slavonia's landscapes are a study in contrasts. The fertile plains, lush forests, and rolling hills of the region make it an ideal location for agriculture. Fields of golden wheat and sunflowers stretch to the horizon, creating a lovely scene that changes with the seasons. On the eastern outskirts of Slavonia is Kopacki Rit, a pristine wetland ecosystem and one of Europe's largest ornithological reserves. This natural wonder is a haven for birdwatchers and those seeking peace in the great outdoors.

Cities that are alive: Slavonia is home to vibrant cities rich in history. Osijek, the region's largest city, draws visitors with its Baroque architecture and the iconic Tvra, an 18th-century fortress. Slavonski Brod is another notable city that combines cultural influences from Austria-Hungary, Croatia, and Serbia. The riverside promenade and the Klasije Monastery are its main draws.

Wine and food: Slavonia's wine culture is well-known. The region's fertile soil supports vineyards that produce high-quality wines, most notably the crisp white wine Graevina. Wine trails wind through picturesque vineyard landscapes, and many local winemakers offer tastings to visitors. With hearty dishes like kulen (spicy sausage), obanac (goulash), and traditional pastries, Slavonian cuisine reflects its agricultural heritage. A local farmstead is the best place to experience Slavonian hospitality, where you can sample authentic dishes and homemade rakija (fruit brandy).

Ethnic Diversity: Slavonia's history has been shaped by a variety of ethnic influences. The region is home to Croatians, Serbs, Hungarians, and Germans, whose traditions, music, and cuisine have woven a rich tapestry of cultural heritage. Don't miss out on Slavonian tamburica music's melodic rhythms or one of the traditional local festivals where you can sample various regional specialties.

A Successful Harvest: Because of its fertile soil and agricultural traditions, Slavonia has become Croatia's breadbasket. Traditional markets abound, offering the chance to try the freshest produce, honey, and homemade preserves. The region's famous paprika from Baranja is an essential ingredient in many local dishes and a popular souvenir for visitors.

Untouched Beauty: The unspoiled beauty of Slavonia is a closely guarded secret. Explore the Akovo region's lush fields, or take a leisurely drive through Slavonia's heart to admire the bucolic charm of its villages. The UNESCO biosphere reserve of Kopacki Rit is a birdwatcher's paradise, with a diverse range of avian species. The unspoiled landscapes offer both nature's serenity and opportunities for outdoor adventures.

Chapter 3: Zagreb: The Capital City

Zagreb, Croatia's vibrant capital, seamlessly blends old-world charm with a modern European vibe. Gornji Grad, the city's historic Upper Town, features medieval streets, colorful facades, and iconic landmarks like St. Mark's Church. Lower Town, on the other hand, is a hive of activity with cafes, museums, and cultural events. Zagreb's art galleries, museums, and festivals weave a rich cultural tapestry. You'll discover a city that values its heritage while embracing modern life as you walk through its vibrant streets, making Zagreb a captivating and dynamic European capital.

Discovering Zagreb

Croatia's heart and capital, Zagreb, embodies the country's rich history, dynamic culture, and modern energy. As you enter this enchanting urban landscape, you're greeted by a city that seamlessly blends its historic past with modern charm, providing a captivating and unforgettable authentic Croatian experience.

The towns of Gornji Grad and Donji Grad are twins:

Zagreb is the story of two cities whose histories are intertwined. Upper Town (Gornji Grad) transports you to a medieval world of narrow cobblestone streets, red-tiled roofs, and colorful facades. At its heart, St. Mark's Church is famous for its iconic roof, which depicts the coats of arms of Croatia, Dalmatia, and Slavonia. The Lotrak Tower, built in the 13th century, stands nearby, guarding Zagreb's rich history.

Lower Town, or Donji Grad, on the other hand, has a more dynamic and modern vibe. Vibrant squares, lively streets, and outdoor cafes set the tone for exploring Zagreb's contemporary cultural scene. The Main Square (Trg bana Jelaia) serves as a focal point, and from there, you can wander through streets lined with boutiques, art galleries, and a variety of culinary delights.

The Cultural Canvas of Zagreb: Museums and Galleries

Zagreb is a cultural treasure trove with something for everyone. Both the Mimara Museum and the Croatian Natural History Museum are must-see attractions. Art lovers will enjoy the Klovievi Dvori Gallery, which features a diverse range of visual arts, while modern creativity will enjoy the Museum of Contemporary Art.

In contrast, the quirky and charming Museum of Broken Relationships truly distinguishes Zagreb. This one-of-a-kind museum collects and displays mementos from failed love affairs, offering a touching and often humorous look at the human condition.

Cafe Culture and Kavana are two examples:

Zagreb's streets are lined with cafes, indicating the city's strong coffee culture. Coffee and people-watching are popular pastimes for both residents and visitors. Cafe culture is deeply embedded in the social fabric of the city, making it an ideal location for relaxation and immersion in the local way of life.

Dolac Market and Culinary Delights:

Visit the bustling Dolac Market to sample Zagreb's culinary scene, where farmers and vendors sell fresh produce, cheeses, and regional specialties. Enjoy traditional dishes like price s minima (turkey with pasta) and truly, a delightful pastry filled with cottage cheese. The city's restaurant scene is thriving, and Zagreb's culinary identity celebrates both local and international flavors.

A Festival and Event Cultural Symphony:

Zagreb values cultural events and festivals. Advent, Zagreb's winter festival, turns the city into a glittering wonderland of lights, music, and seasonal charm. One of the region's largest open-air music festivals, the INmusic Festival, draws music fans from all over Europe.

Must-See Sights

Croatia's vibrant capital, Zagreb, has a plethora of must-see attractions that reflect the city's rich history and vibrant culture. These attractions, which include everything from historic landmarks to lively squares and captivating museums, provide a glimpse into Zagreb's diverse identity.

Ban Jelai Square: As the heart of Zagreb's central meeting place, Ban Jelai Square is an excellent place to start your exploration. The square is ringed by cafes and shops, and the equestrian statue of Ban Josip Jelai, a revered Croatian leader, towers over it. It is the city's focal point.

St. Mark's Church: Located in Zagreb's charming Upper Town, St. Mark's Church is a city symbol. Its colorful tiled roof, which features Croatian, Dalmatian, and Slavic coats of arms, is a timeless image. There are exquisite Gothic sculptures inside.

Upper Town (Gornji Grad): This historic district transports you back in time with its medieval streets, enchanting architecture, and charming courtyards. For panoramic views, go to the Stone Gate (Kamenita vrata), which houses a miraculous painting of the Virgin Mary, and Lotrak Tower.

The Museum of Broken Relationships is an affecting look at failed love affairs. It exhibits personal objects and stories from people all over the world, resulting in an emotional and frequently humorous experience.

Zagreb Cathedral: The towering twin spires of Zagreb Cathedral dominate the city's skyline. The interior of this neo-Gothic masterpiece is equally impressive, with intricate frescoes and stunning stained glass windows.

Dolac Market: The lively farmers' market in Zagreb, Dolac, is a sensory overload. Fresh produce, regional specialties, and artisanal goods abound at the market stalls. It's an excellent place to try traditional Croatian cuisine and learn about the local culinary culture.

Klovievi Dvori Gallery: This visual arts gallery has a large collection of works by well-known Croatian artists. Its hilltop location provides panoramic views of the city.

Mirogoj Cemetery: With arcades, chapels, and lush greenery, Mirogoj Cemetery is a stunning architectural gem. It's both a tranquil haven and an open-air art and history museum.

Jarun Lake: For outdoor enthusiasts, Jarun Lake is a recreational haven. You can swim, sail, bike, or simply relax by the water. It is a popular spot for recreation and sports among the locals.

Advent in Zagreb: If you're in town during the winter, don't miss Advent in Zagreb. With dazzling lights, holiday markets, ice skating rinks, and a heartwarming festive atmosphere, the city comes alive.

Culinary Delights

Croatia's capital, Zagreb, has a diverse and delicious culinary scene. The city's restaurants, cafes, and food markets cater to a wide range of tastes, from traditional Croatian dishes to international flavors, promising a gastronomic journey to delight your palate.

The best of Croatian cuisine: Start your culinary adventure with traditional Croatian dishes. The cuisine's heart is comprised of locally sourced ingredients, resulting in hearty and flavorful dishes. Try the "truly," a savory pastry filled with cottage cheese and sour cream, and the "public s minima," a turkey and flatbread dish. Local favorites include "kulen," a spicy sausage, and "zagrebaki break," a breaded and fried veal or pork cutlet filled with ham and cheese.

Peka and fresh seafood: Restaurants in Zagreb serve fresh seafood from the Adriatic. A must-try is the "Crni riot," or black risotto, made with squid ink, rice, and seafood. There is also a selection of grilled fish and seafood, which is frequently prepared with local olive oil and aromatic herbs. Order the "peak," a slow-cooked meat or seafood with vegetables beneath a bell-shaped lid.

Coffee Culture: Zagreb has a vibrant coffee culture that is deeply ingrained in the city's social fabric. The streets are lined with cafes and kavanas (coffeehouses), inviting you to sip your coffee while taking in the atmosphere. Take your time instead, and enjoy a leisurely cup of coffee while people-watching in one of the many cozy cafes.

Markets that sell fresh produce: Dolac Market is an excellent place to sample the freshest local produce. Here you'll find an abundance of fruits, vegetables, cheeses, and homemade products. Try regional specialties like "kulen," a spicy sausage, as well as homemade jams and preserves. This market is a culinary delight, offering insight into the agricultural traditions of the region.

Flavors from All Over the World: Because of Zagreb's multiculturalism, a diverse range of international cuisine is readily available. You can sample a variety of flavors, including Italian and Mediterranean fare as well as Asian and Middle Eastern fare. From gourmet burgers to sushi and curry, the city's diverse restaurant scene has something for everyone.

Bakeries and desserts: Remember to treat yourself to something sweet. Bakeries in Zagreb sell pastries such as "krafne" (doughnuts) and "trudla" (strudel). In addition, there are several delightful dessert shops in the city where you can indulge in delectable cakes, chocolates, and ice cream.

The culinary landscape of Zagreb combines tradition and innovation, resulting in a delectable fusion of flavors to please every palate.

Chapter 4: The Adriatic Coast

The Adriatic Coast of Croatia is a breathtaking stretch of coastline on the Adriatic Sea's eastern shore. This lovely coastal region is known for its crystal-clear waters, picturesque islands, and historic towns. The coastline is dotted with remarkable destinations, ranging from Dubrovnik's stunning city walls to Split's vibrant port. Relax on pebble beaches, visit charming fishing villages, and sample Mediterranean cuisine. The Adriatic Coast is a cultural and natural treasure trove that embodies Croatia's beauty and hospitality.

Coastal Highlights

The Adriatic Coast of Croatia is a rich tapestry of breathtaking landscapes, historic towns, and sun-kissed beaches. This Mediterranean treasure has a plethora of coastal highlights, making it a popular destination for visitors looking for natural beauty, rich culture, and unforgettable experiences.

The Adriatic Pearl: Dubrovnik, known as the "Pearl of the Adriatic," is a historical and elegant city. Its well-preserved old town is a UNESCO World Heritage site, surrounded by ancient city walls. Discover the marble streets, the city walls, and landmarks like the Rector's Palace and the Franciscan Monastery. The allure of Dubrovnik is enhanced by its dramatic coastal setting and the glistening Adriatic Sea.

Split - Where History Meets the Sea: Split, Croatia's second-largest city, blends ancient history with a vibrant Mediterranean lifestyle. At its heart is Diocletian's Palace, an impressive Roman structure that now serves as the city's historic center. Stroll through the palace's charming alleyways, see the Peristyle, and unwind on the Riva, Split's waterfront promenade. The city's unique blend of history and modern culture creates an unforgettable coastal experience.

Paradise Island - Hvar: Hvar is a well-known Croatian island known for its lavender fields, vineyards, and lively nightlife. Hvar is a must-see for its elegant architecture and historic squares. Explore the 13th-century walls of Hvar Fortress, sip local wine at nearby vineyards, and relax on the island's idyllic beaches. Hvar's allure extends from its historic past to its modern vibrancy.

Korula, a Medieval Masterpiece: Korula Island is frequently compared to a miniature Dubrovnik due to its medieval architecture and city walls. Korula, thought to be Marco Polo's birthplace, is a magnificent example of a well-preserved historic center. Visit St. Mark's Cathedral and see the traditional Moreska sword dance. The beautiful beaches and peaceful atmosphere of the island add to its allure.

Zadar - An Old and New Fusion: Zadar, on Croatia's northern coast, is a one-of-a-kind coastal destination that combines ancient history and modern art installations. Explore the Roman Forum and St. Donatus Church before seeing the Sea Organ and Sun Salutation, two contemporary art installations along the waterfront. Zadar's Adriatic charm offers a diverse cultural experience.

Rovinj is an Istrian beauty: Rovinj is a picturesque Istrian Peninsula coastal town with a strong Venetian influence. Its old town, with its narrow cobblestone streets and pastel-colored buildings, is a joy to explore. Climb to the top of St. Euphemia's Basilica for panoramic views and dine at one of the city's charming waterside restaurants. Rovinj is a coastal jewel because of its romantic allure and seaside allure.

The Adriatic Coast of Croatia is a treasure trove of coastal highlights, each with its unique personality and charm. From the historic grandeur of Dubrovnik to the island paradise of Hvar and the artistic innovation of Zadar, this coastal region offers a rich tapestry of experiences that capture the essence of Croatia's Mediterranean allure.

Dubrovnik: The Pearl of the Adriatic

Dubrovnik, Croatia's stunning Dalmatian coast, is known as the "Pearl of the Adriatic," and it enchants visitors with its rich history, architectural splendor, and breathtaking coastal setting. This coastal jewel is a UNESCO World Heritage site and a popular tourist destination for people from all over the world.

A City Rich in History: The well-preserved medieval old town of Dubrovnik is surrounded by imposing city walls that have stood the test of time. These massive fortifications, with their distinctive terracotta roofs, make an impressive first impression while protecting the treasures within.

The Stradun Historic District: Walking down the main street, Stradun is like stepping back in time. It winds through the picturesque old town, which is lined with historic buildings as well as lively shops and cafes. Highlights include the Rector's Palace, the Sponza Palace, and the Franciscan Monastery, which houses one of Europe's oldest operating pharmacies. Explore the streets to find hidden squares and charming churches.

Fortifications and city defenses: Dubrovnik's city walls are among the best preserved in the world. A stroll along these walls provides stunning views of the city, the Adriatic Sea, and the surrounding islands. Fortresses such as the Minceta Tower and the Lovrijenac Fortress, which served as both defensive structures and iconic landmarks, can be found strategically placed throughout the city.

Culture's Delights: Dubrovnik's cultural scene is equally captivating. In the city, numerous art galleries, including the Dubrovnik Art Gallery and the War Photo Limited, present powerful exhibitions. The open-air Dubrovnik Summer Festival, which takes place in a variety of historic venues, also features live performances.

The Adriatic Coast: Dubrovnik's coastal setting adds to its allure. The Adriatic Sea, with its crystal-clear waters, frames the city and offers opportunities for swimming, snorkeling, and boat trips to nearby islands. Banje Beach, a short walk from the old town, is a popular spot for sunbathing and swimming.

Culinary Arts Achievement: Dubrovnik cuisine is a delectable journey through Mediterranean flavors. Fresh seafood, olive oil, and local herbs are frequently used in its dishes. Try the catch of the day at a seaside restaurant, savor Dalmatian specialties like black risotto, and indulge in sweet treats like "rota," a caramel custard dessert.

Dubrovnik during Christmas: Visiting Dubrovnik during Advent, the city's festive winter market is a once-in-a-lifetime opportunity. The old town transforms into a winter wonderland with beautifully decorated streets, an ice skating rink, and a plethora of holiday stalls.

The Pearl's Legacies: Despite earthquakes and wars, Dubrovnik's enduring allure reflects the city's resilience and determination to preserve its cultural heritage. The resilience and dedication to preserving the "Pearl of the Adriatic" exemplify the essence of the "Pearl of the Adriatic."

Dubrovnik, the "Pearl of the Adriatic," transports you through time with its magnificent old town, historic grandeur, and coastal beauty. It's a destination that combines history, culture, and natural beauty, promising an unforgettable journey into the Mediterranean heart of Croatia.

Split: Ancient History and Modern Vibes

Split, Croatia's second-largest city, is an enthralling destination that blends ancient history with a vibrant Mediterranean lifestyle. This Dalmatian coast coastal jewel provides a one-of-a-kind experience, combining historic sites, breathtaking nature, and contemporary culture to create an enchanting urban landscape.

The Diocletian's Palace as a Living Museum: Diocletian's Palace, the retirement residence of a Roman emperor in the fourth century, is located in the heart of Split. This well-preserved palace complex is a UNESCO World Heritage site and an integral part of Split's identity. Learn about the palace's rich history by exploring the ancient alleyways, marveling at the Peristyle, and exploring the underground chambers.

The Riva and City Life: The Riva, or waterfront promenade, is at the epicenter of the city's modern buzz. Because it is lined with cafes, restaurants, and palm trees, it is the ideal place to enjoy a coffee or gelato while taking in the local atmosphere. The lively ambiance of The Riva reflects Split's dynamic urban lifestyle.

Landmarks and Historic Attractions: Split, aside from Diocletian's Palace, is rich in historical landmarks. The Cathedral of Saint Domnius, formerly Diocletian's mausoleum, is a magnificent example of Romanesque architecture. A must-see is the bell tower, which can be climbed for panoramic views. The Temple of Jupiter is another nearby historic treasure, and the Prokurative Square is a grand ensemble of neoclassical buildings.

Cultural festivals and events: The cultural scene in Split is alive and well all year. Split Summer Festival includes theater, opera, and concerts in historic venues like Peristyle. Ultra Europe, Europe's largest electronic dance music festival, attracts music enthusiasts from around the world. Throughout the year, galleries and exhibitions bring the artistic spirit of the city to life.

Marjan Hill is a natural oasis: For a nature escape in the heart of the city, head to Marjan Hill. This forested park provides hiking trails, stunning views, and a peaceful escape from the city. You can also go swimming and sunbathing on the beautiful Marjan peninsula and its beaches.

Beaches and Water Sports: Split's coastline is dotted with beaches that offer relaxation and aquatic activities. Swimming and the traditional game of picnic are popular activities at Bavice Beach. Ovice and Firule are two other urban beaches, while Trstenik and Znjan are more secluded.

Various Cuisines: The culinary scene in Split blends Mediterranean and Dalmatian influences. The stars of the show are fresh seafood, olive oil, and local herbs. Try "pasticada," a traditional Dalmatian dish, or "gregada," a fish stew. Pair your meals with local wines or a light Dalmatian white wine like "Vugava."

Boating and island hopping: Split's strategic coastal location makes it an ideal base for exploring the surrounding islands. On a boat trip to Bra, Hvar, or Vis, you can enjoy pristine beaches, historic towns, and island culture.

Split is an enthralling contrast of ancient history and modern vibes. Its ancient palace and historic landmarks coexist peacefully with its vibrant urban culture, resulting in a destination where you can learn about history, enjoy the Mediterranean lifestyle, and marvel at the natural beauty of the Dalmatian coast.

Chapter 5: Islands and Beaches

Croatia's coast is an island and beach haven. With over a thousand islands scattered along the Adriatic Sea, it offers a diverse range of coastal beauty. From the bustling beaches of Hvar to the tranquil coves of Vis and the unspoiled landscapes of Cres, each island has its personality. Swimming and sunbathing are ideal on Croatia's pebble and sandy beaches, such as Zlatni Rat on Bra and Baka on Krk. With their crystal-clear waters, sheltered coves, and abundant marine life, these coastal gems entice beachgoers and nature enthusiasts alike.

Choosing Your Island Paradise

Croatia's beautiful coastline is dotted with islands, each of which offers a unique slice of Mediterranean paradise. There are numerous islands to choose from for your Croatian vacation, ranging from bustling tourist hotspots to tranquil, off-the-beaten-path gems. Let's take a look at how to pick your Croatian island paradise.

The Glitzy Gem of Hvar: If you want to experience natural beauty, history, and vibrant nightlife, Hvar is the place to be. With its lavender fields, olive groves, and crystal-clear waters, this island captures the essence of

Dalmatia. Hvar Town, with its medieval streets and vibrant squares, is well-known for its nightlife. Visit the charming Stari Grad and Jelsa for a more relaxed atmosphere.

Beach Lovers' Paradise Bra: The bra is an excellent choice for those looking for beautiful beaches and a relaxing atmosphere. It is the location of the well-known Zlatni Rat Beach, also known as the Golden Horn. Sunbathers flock to this pebble beach because of its unique shape and crystal-clear waters. Aside from the beach, you can explore the picturesque town of Bol, sip local wines, and savor the culinary delights of the island.

Korula - A Historical Icon: Korula, a mini-Dubrovnik, is a medieval gem with well-preserved walls and historic streets. It is thought that explorer Marco Polo was born here. Korula is ideal for history buffs who want to wander the winding streets, visit St. Mark's Cathedral, and watch the traditional Moreska sword dance.

Private Retreat - Vis: Vis is a peaceful hideaway perfect for those looking for a peaceful escape. The island was a military outpost for many years, which kept it off the tourist radar. It now offers unspoiled landscapes, peaceful villages, and stunning beaches like Stiniva. Explore Vis Town, the stunning Blue Cave on nearby Bievo Island, and the island's seafood and wine.

Pag - Party Site: Pag is famous for its wild nightlife, especially in Novalja, which is home to Zre Beach, a popular location for electronic music festivals. The island, however, has more to offer than just parties. It is known for its distinct landscape, which includes rocky terrain, salt pans, and a unique cheese known as "Paki sir," as well as the peaceful town of Pag and the island's cultural heritage.

Krk - Family-Friendly Entertainment: Krk, Croatia's largest island, is an excellent choice for families. A bridge connects the island to the mainland. Krk has a variety of beaches, historical towns like Krk and Baka, and activities for people of all ages. Biserujka Cave is a one-of-a-kind underground attraction in the Vrbnik region, which is well-known for its wine production.

Natural Paradise Mljet: Mljet, part of the Mljet National Park, is a nature lover's dream. It has a dense forest and two saltwater lakes, Malo Jezero and Veliko Jezero, where you can swim and kayak. The island also has a Benedictine monastery on an islet in the middle of one of the lakes. Mljet is an ideal destination for those looking for peace and natural beauty.

Cres Natural Beauty: Cres, the largest island in the northern Adriatic, is a lovely and tranquil getaway. Its landscape ranges from rugged cliffs to lush forests and peaceful coves. Explore the medieval town of Cres and sample the local cuisine, particularly lamb and seafood. Cres is a hidden treasure for an authentic off-the-beaten-path experience.

Korula - A Historical Icon: Korula, a mini-Dubrovnik, is a medieval gem with well-preserved walls and historic streets. It is thought that explorer Marco Polo was born here. Korula is ideal for history buffs who want to wander the winding streets, visit St. Mark's Cathedral, and watch the traditional Moreska sword dance.

Alta - Regional Appeal: Alta, a tranquil island near Split, provides a welcome respite from the crowds. The island's pace of life is slow, with traditional fishing villages and beautiful bays for swimming and sunbathing. The main towns, Maslinica and Grohote, provide a taste of local life and cuisine.

When choosing your island paradise in Croatia, think about the type of experience you want. Croatia's islands have it all: vibrant nightlife, historic charm, peaceful nature, and authentic local flavor. Your ideal island awaits, ready to provide an unforgettable Mediterranean vacation.

Beaches and Water Activities

The stunning Adriatic Sea coastline of Croatia is a paradise for beachgoers and watersports enthusiasts. With its crystal-clear waters, idyllic islands, and diverse range of beaches, the country provides a coastal paradise for relaxation and adventure.

Everyone Can Enjoy the Beach: Croatia has a diverse range of beaches to suit all tastes. From pebble beaches like Zlatni Rat on Bra, which offers a unique shifting shape due to changing currents, to sandy havens like Baka Beach on Krk Island, where soft sands meet the sea, there's a beach for everyone. Secluded coves on Vis Island, such as Stiniva Beach, provide privacy and tranquility, whereas urban beaches, such as Dubrovnik's Banje Beach, provide a vibrant seaside atmosphere.

There are numerous water activities available: The pristine waters of the Adriatic Sea invite a variety of water activities. Due to the abundance of underwater caves, shipwrecks, and vibrant marine life to explore, snorkeling and diving are popular activities. Kayaking allows you to paddle along the coast, discover hidden coves, and relax in the sea's tranquility.

Sailing and island hopping: Croatia is a sailor's paradise, with thousands of islands. By chartering a yacht or joining a sailing tour, you can discover the Adriatic's hidden gems. By island hopping, you can visit picturesque villages, sample local cuisine, and learn about historic sites.

Windsurfing and kiteboarding: Windsurfing and kiteboarding are both thrilling activities for thrill seekers. Locations such as Bol on Bra and the Peljeac Peninsula provide strong winds and suitable conditions for these high-energy sports.

Exciting Cliff Diving: The dramatic coastline and cliffs of the Dalmatian coast make for an ideal setting for cliff diving. Daring adventurers can take breathtaking leaps into the Adriatic at some local spots, such as the cliffs near Dubrovnik or the Blue Hole on Vis Island.

Cruises and Sea Tours: Cruises and sea tours are fantastic ways to explore the country's breathtaking coastline, archipelagos, and hidden treasures. Boat trips to the Blue Cave on Bievo Island or the Elafiti Islands near Dubrovnik show off Croatia's natural beauty.

Stand-Up Paddleboarding (SUP): Stand-up paddleboarding is gaining popularity along Croatia's coast. Rent a board and cruise through the calm bays, inlets, and clear waters at your leisure. SUP is a relaxing way to connect with nature and enjoy the scenery.

Fishing and seafood experiences: Fishermen can either join local fishermen on their daily excursions or book their fishing trips. It's a chance to experiment with traditional fishing techniques and enjoy the catch of the day. Seafood lovers can enjoy fresh and delicious Adriatic-inspired dishes at local restaurants.

Unknown Coves Swimming: One of the pleasures of the Croatian coast is discovering hidden coves and inlets ideal for swimming and sunbathing. Many of these hidden gems are only accessible by boat, providing a peaceful respite from the crowds.

Island-Hopping Itineraries

The promise of diverse experiences, historical riches, and natural beauty entices visitors to Croatia's coast, which is dotted with over a thousand islands. Island-hopping itineraries are a great way to explore this coastal wonderland, whether you're a history buff, an adventure seeker, or a beach lover.

1. Dalmatian Customs:

The starting point is split.

Popular tourist destinations include Hvar, Bra, Vis, Korula, and Olta.

Begin your journey in Split, where you can see Diocletian's Palace and stroll along the lively Riva promenade. Travel to the glamorous island of Hvar to enjoy its vibrant nightlife. Continue to Bra, which is famous for its Zlatni Rat Beach. Vis, with its hidden coves and the enthralling Blue Cave, offers a more peaceful escape. Korula, with its medieval charm and historical significance, is another must-see. Finish your journey with a relaxing retreat on the peaceful island of Olta.

2. Northern Natural Wonders:

Zadar serves as the starting point.

Popular tourist destinations include Pag, Rab, Krk, Cres, and Loinj.

Zadar, with its Sea Organ and Sun Salutation, is your starting point. Pag, known for its wild nightlife and distinctive landscapes, is the next stop on your island-hopping adventure. Rab has historic beauty and beautiful beaches, and it is followed by the vibrant island of Krk, which is accessible by bridge. Cres enchants with its pristine nature, and your journey can end on the lush and green island of Loinj.

3. The Southern Serenity:

The starting point is Dubrovnik.

Popular tourist destinations include Mljet, Lastovo, Ipan, and Lopud.

Dubrovnik's Old Town is an ideal starting point due to its historic charm and beauty. Mljet National Park is known for its lush greenery and tranquil lakes. Continue to Lastovo, an unspoiled island with picturesque villages. The Elafiti Islands' ipan and Lopud offer beautiful scenery and peace.

4. The Cultural Isthmus:

Pula serves as the starting point.

Brijuni, Loinj, and Cres are popular vacation spots.

Pula's Roman heritage and the impressive Arena Amphitheater will be your first cultural encounters. Brijuni Islands are a historical treasure, rich in history and pristine in nature. Continue to Loinj and Cres for a peaceful combination of beautiful scenery and charming towns.

5. Expedition to the Kornati Archipelago:

Zadar serves as the starting point.

The islands of Kornati National Park are popular tourist destinations.

This itinerary focuses on the Kornati Archipelago, a national park made up of numerous islands and islets. You'll travel to this untouched natural wonder known for its rocky landscapes, crystal-clear waters, and abundant marine life, beginning in Zadar. It's a haven for sailors and nature lovers.

6. The Istrian Retreat:

As a starting point, consider Pula or Rijeka.

Popular tourist destinations include Loinj, Cres, Rab, and Krk.

Begin your journey in Pula or Rijeka and travel to the Loinj and Cres islands. From there, explore the historic and charming island of Rab. Continue to Krk, which is known for its easy accessibility and diverse landscapes. It's a route that highlights the cultural and natural diversity of the Istrian coast.

Chapter 6: History and Culture

Croatia's rich history and vibrant culture are woven into the fabric of the country. Croatia has a diverse historical heritage, ranging from the ancient Roman ruins of Diocletian's Palace in Split to the medieval charm of Dubrovnik's Old Town. Local folklore and traditional dances provide insight into the country's cultural identity, while festivals and museums honor its art and music traditions. Croatian cuisine reflects its historical tapestry, with influences from the Mediterranean and Eastern Europe. Visitors have proudly shared the country's strong sense of tradition and deeply rooted customs, making it an enthralling destination for history and culture enthusiasts.

Croatia's Rich History

Croatia's history, spanning from ancient Roman times to the modern era, is an enthralling story of resilience, transformation, and influence. This coastal jewel of southeastern Europe has seen empires rise and fall, leaving a legacy of cultural diversity and historical landmarks.

Antiquity and the Roman Legacy: Croatia's history begins with the conquest of the country by the Romans in the first century BC, when it became a part of the Roman Empire. The most enduring symbol of this era is Diocletian's Palace in Split, a magnificent UNESCO World Heritage site built by Emperor Diocletian himself. The well-preserved remains of the palace attest to the magnificence of Roman architecture and engineering.

The Byzantine Stamp: Croatia was conquered by the Byzantines in the sixth century, following the fall of the Western Roman Empire. The Byzantine influence can be seen in Croatian art and architecture, particularly in the early Christian basilicas scattered throughout the country.

Middle Ages Kingdoms and Empires: During the Middle Ages, Croatia evolved from a collection of small kingdoms and duchies into a unified medieval kingdom, culminating in the coronation of King Tomislav in 925. Croatian cities such as Dubrovnik and Trogir flourished as cultural and commercial centers during this period.

Ottoman and Venetian Empires: Croatia was a prized possession for various empires due to its strategic location along the Adriatic. Venetian rule forever altered the coastal towns, while parts of the country, particularly Slavonia, fell under Ottoman control. The Venetian architecture of cities like Rovinj and Dubrovnik reflects this era.

The Habsburg Monarchy and the Austro-Hungarian Empire: Croatia's fortunes shifted once more with the Habsburg monarchy and, later, the Austro-Hungarian Empire, bringing political stability and economic development. During this period, the capital, Zagreb, emerged as a vibrant cultural and political center.

Yugoslavia's Kingdom and the Troubled Twentieth Century: Croatia became a member of the Kingdom of Yugoslavia in the early twentieth century. The aftermath of World War I, as well as the interwar instability, culminated in World War II, causing significant upheaval and transformation in Croatia.

The Declaration of Independence and the War for Independence: Croatia declared independence from Yugoslavia in 1991, triggering the brutal Homeland War. The Croatian people's perseverance during this difficult period is an important part of the country's modern history.

A Vibrant Modern Republic: Croatia emerged as an independent republic following the Homeland War, and it has thrived as a democratic nation ever since. The country has worked tirelessly to preserve its historical heritage and showcase its cultural richness through museums, festivals, and a strong commitment to preserving its unique cultural identity.

Cultural Heritage and Museums

Croatia's cultural heritage is a vibrant tapestry woven from the threads of its diverse history, including influences from the Roman Empire, the Byzantine era, Venetian rule, the Austro-Hungarian Empire, and others. The country's rich history is vividly preserved in its numerous museums, where visitors can embark on a fascinating journey through time.

The Archaeological Museums:

Croatia's archaeological museums are portals to the past. The Archaeological Museum in Zagreb houses a remarkable collection of artifacts dating from the Neanderthal era to the Middle Ages. Split's Archaeological Museum displays the heritage of the Roman colony of Salona as well as other historical periods. Pula's Archaeological Museum, housed in an Austro-Hungarian fortress, displays Roman relics and prehistoric treasures.

Ethnographic and historical museums:

Croatia's historical museums capture the essence of its diverse past. The Museum of Croatian Archaeological Monuments in Split houses an impressive collection of medieval artifacts. The Museum of Slavonia in Osijek focuses on the history of Slavonia and Baranja, whereas the Museum of Meimurje in Akovec explores the heritage of the northern region.

Art Galleries and Museums:

Croatia's art museums and galleries are a veritable treasure trove of creativity. The Museum of Contemporary Art in Zagreb houses a large collection of modern and contemporary art, while the Museum of Arts and Crafts focuses on applied arts and design. The Gallery of Fine Arts in Split houses works ranging from the Renaissance to the twentieth century.

Maritime Museums:

Given Croatia's extensive coastline, maritime heritage plays an important role in its culture. The Maritime and History Museum of the Croatian Littoral in Rijeka provides an insight into the Adriatic's maritime history. Split's Maritime Museum focuses on the city's naval history, while Pula's Archaeological and Maritime Museum investigates underwater archaeology.

Unique museums:

Croatia is home to some extraordinary and one-of-a-kind museums. The Museum of Broken Relationships in Zagreb tells moving stories through donated mementos from previous relationships. The Froggyland Museum in Split is a quirky collection of taxidermy frogs posed in amusing scenes. The Museum of Illusions, also in Zagreb, is a fun and interactive experience that challenges perception.

UNESCO World Heritage Sites:

Croatia has several UNESCO World Heritage Sites, including the historic city of Dubrovnik, which is known for its remarkably well-preserved city walls and medieval architecture. The Euphrasian Basilica in Pore, with its stunning mosaics, is another UNESCO World Heritage Site. In Split, Diocletian's Palace, a living monument, is an important part of the city's heritage.

Croatia's Intangible Heritage:

Croatia's cultural heritage extends beyond museums. The country celebrates its intangible heritage through festivals, music, dance, and traditions. The Sinjska Alka, a knights' tournament in Sinj, is a UNESCO-recognized tradition. Another aspect of Croatian cultural heritage is the polyphonic singing of the Klapa, a type of vocal music.

Cultural Festivals:

Croatia hosts a plethora of cultural festivals throughout the year to showcase its artistic diversity. The Dubrovnik Summer Festival, held in the city's historic venues, includes theater, opera, and concerts. The Motovun Film Festival celebrates independent and alternative cinema. In Varadin, the Pacifist is a lively street festival that combines culture and entertainment.

Festivals and Events

Croatia is a country that knows how to celebrate its rich cultural heritage and diverse traditions. Throughout the year, the country hosts a plethora of festivals and events that bring together music, arts, history, and the vibrant spirit of its people. Whether you enjoy music, and history, or simply want to immerse yourself in the local culture, Croatia has a wide range of festivals to offer.

1. Dubrovnik Summer Festival: This renowned cultural event is held in the historic city of Dubrovnik and takes place in the city's most iconic venues, including the grand Rector's Palace and the open-air Revelin Fortress. The festival features an enthralling lineup of theater performances, classical music concerts, and opera, attracting both locals and visitors to celebrate the arts in a truly magical setting.

2. Pancirfest, Varadin: Pancirfest is one of Croatia's most dynamic street festivals, transforming the picturesque town of Varadin into a vibrant hub of arts, music, and entertainment. Stroll through the cobblestone streets and enjoy live music, street performers, art exhibitions, and culinary delights. The festival's lively atmosphere reflects Croatia's commitment to fostering cultural experiences.

3. Motovun Film Festival: This one-of-a-kind film festival, held in the hilltop town of Motovun, has gained international recognition for showcasing independent and alternative cinema. The festival's stunning setting, nestled among the vineyards of Istria, provides a memorable backdrop for cinematic exploration. It's a cultural gathering that appeals to film fans looking for innovative and thought-provoking works.

4. Sinjska Alka, Sinj: Sinjska Alka is a centuries-old tradition celebrated with a knights' tournament in Sinj. This event, recognized by UNESCO as an intangible cultural heritage, is a spectacular display of equestrian skills, historical reenactments, and traditional clothing. It is a living testament to Croatia's rich heritage and martial history.

5. Dubrovnik Carnival: Croatia's annual carnival season is filled with colorful parades, masked balls, and lively festivities. The Dubrovnik Carnival is a particularly vibrant celebration, with participants dressed in elaborate costumes parading through the city's ancient streets. The celebration combines historical traditions with modern revelry.

6. Dubrovnik St. Blaise Festival: This festival honors St. Blaise, Dubrovnik's patron saint. Processions, religious ceremonies, and cultural events are all part of the festivities. One of the highlights is the release of white doves, which represent peace and freedom. The festival embodies the deep spiritual connection that is woven into Croatia's cultural fabric.

7. International Folklore Festival in Zagreb: The International Folklore Festival in Zagreb celebrates the world's diverse cultural heritage. Folk dance groups from all over the world gather to share their traditional music,

dance, and customs. The event promotes cross-cultural understanding and emphasizes the importance of preserving and celebrating global traditions.

8. Pula Film Festival: Pula's film festival is one of the most prestigious in Croatia, showcasing national and international cinematic works. The festival, held in the magnificent Roman amphitheater, adds a touch of historical charm to contemporary cinema. It's a film festival that combines art and heritage.

Chapter 7: Outdoor Adventures

Croatia's diverse landscapes make it a haven for outdoor enthusiasts. Hikers can explore the rugged beauty of Plitvice Lakes National Park or the dramatic cliffs of Paklenica National Park. The country's numerous rivers provide opportunities for thrilling white-water rafting, while the clear Adriatic waters are ideal for scuba diving and snorkeling. Croatia's islands are a sailing and windsurfing paradise, and rock climbers will find challenging routes in Paklenica and on the island of Hvar. Cycling along scenic coastal paths or taking a leisurely kayak trip are popular options for those looking for a more relaxed outdoor experience, ensuring there's something for everyone.

Hiking and National Parks

Croatia's natural beauty is on full display in its national parks, which offer a plethora of hiking opportunities. The country's national parks are a paradise for outdoor enthusiasts, with everything from cascading waterfalls and pristine lakes to lush forests and dramatic cliffs.

1. Plitvice Lakes National Park: Plitvice Lakes is one of Croatia's most famous national parks, known for its

spectacular series of cascading lakes and waterfalls. The park's well-kept hiking trails wind through lush forests and past crystal-clear lakes. The park's beautiful landscapes are easily explored thanks to wooden boardwalks and bridges. The two main sections are the Lower Lakes and Upper Lakes, each with its distinct personality. The natural beauty of the park is a testament to the enchantment of water and time.

2. Paklenica National Park: Paklenica, located in the Velebit mountain range, is a hiker and climber's paradise. The park's varied terrain includes dramatic limestone canyons, rocky peaks, and dense forests. There are numerous hiking trails suitable for hikers of various skill levels. The Ania Kuk cliff is a popular rock climbing location. The park is also rich in flora and fauna, making it an appealing destination for nature lovers.

3. Krka National Park: Krka National Park is famous for its cascading waterfalls and emerald-green pools. The park's well-kept trails allow visitors to explore the lush landscapes surrounding the Krka River. Skradinski Buk, a beautiful waterfall with a network of wooden walkways and bridges, is one of the highlights. Krka's waterfalls are not only a sight to behold, but also an invitation to a refreshing swim, making it a one-of-a-kind hiking destination.

4. Brijuni National Park: The Brijuni Islands are a hidden gem known for their stunning landscapes and historical sites. Hiking on the islands reveals a mix of Mediterranean vegetation, archaeological treasures, and exotic animal species. The park includes 14 islands, but Veli Brijun and Mali Brijun are the most accessible and visited. Explore the Roman ruins, safari park, and golf course while taking in the breathtaking scenery.

5. Risnjak National Park: Risnjak is a mountainous national park that stands in stark contrast to Croatia's coastal beauty. The park is well-known for its dense forests, high peaks, and diverse wildlife. Hikers can explore the park's well-marked trails that lead to the summit of Mount Risnjak, which offers panoramic views of the surrounding landscape. The park is also home to the elusive lynx, which adds an element of wildlife adventure to your hike.

6. Mljet National Park: Mljet, one of Croatia's Adriatic islands, has a national park that covers the majority of the island. The park is well-known for its two saltwater lakes, Veliko and Malo Jezero. Hiking around the lakes and exploring the picturesque islet of St. Mary is a peaceful outdoor experience. The park's unique combination of lush landscapes and tranquil waters provides a welcome respite.

Sailing the Adriatic

Sailing the Adriatic Sea along Croatia's stunning coast is a seafaring enthusiast's dream. Croatia is a nautical paradise because of its crystal-clear waters, numerous islands, and rich maritime heritage. Here's a look at the incredible experience of sailing this beautiful stretch of the Mediterranean.

Delight in Island-Hopping: Croatia has over a thousand islands, each with its distinct charm. Sailing allows you to explore the archipelago at your own pace. From the bustling shores of Hvar to the tranquil coves of Vis, you'll encounter a diverse range of landscapes and cultures. Sailing allows access to hidden gems that are often only accessible by boat, creating a sense of adventure and exclusivity.

Waters that are crystal clear: The Adriatic's pristine waters are not only a sight to behold but also an invitation to dive in and enjoy swimming and snorkeling. Anchor in secluded bays and coves surrounded by unspoiled nature and cool off in the turquoise sea. The underwater world is teeming with marine life, making it a snorkel and scuba diver's paradise.

Historic Ports and Locations: Croatia's historic coastal towns and cities offer a unique blend of history and modernity. Sail into Dubrovnik, known as the "Pearl of the Adriatic," and explore its well-preserved city walls and old town. Trogir, another UNESCO World Heritage site, welcomes sailors with its medieval charm. Zadar's modern Sea Organ and Sun Salutation installations are a captivating fusion of ancient and contemporary.

Marine Hospitality: Croatia's coastline is dotted with marinas and harbors, making it easy for sailors to dock and explore the mainland. Many of these ports have excellent amenities, such as restaurants, shops, and shower facilities. The warmth and hospitality of the Croatian people add to the overall sailing experience.

Routes and Itineraries: Sailing Croatia provides a variety of routes to choose from, depending on your preferences. The Dalmatian coast, with iconic destinations such as Split, Hvar, and Korula, is a classic choice. The Kornati Archipelago, with its dramatic landscapes and numerous islands, is a sailing paradise for experienced sailors. You can also visit the Istrian peninsula, the northern Adriatic, or the southern Elafiti Islands.

Mediterranean flavors: Croatia's culinary scene is heavily influenced by Mediterranean and Balkan flavors. While sailing, you can stop at picturesque fishing villages and waterfront restaurants to sample fresh seafood, local wines, and regional dishes. Enjoy the catch of the day in the tranquil setting of a coastal konoba (tavern).

Sailing Competitions and Regattas: Croatia hosts a variety of sailing events and regattas, making it an ideal destination for those looking to test their sailing skills or spectate. During these events, the Adriatic coast comes to life, with colorful sails dotting the horizon and lively celebrations on land.

Water Sports and Activities

Croatia's stunning coastline and crystal-clear waters make it an ideal destination for a variety of water sports and activities. From adrenaline-pumping adventures to peaceful aquatic explorations, the country has something for everyone looking to make a splash.

1. Snorkeling and diving: Croatia's underwater world is a treasure trove of marine life, underwater caves, and shipwrecks just waiting to be discovered. Snorkelers will find pristine spots along the coast, while certified divers can explore the Adriatic Sea's captivating mysteries.

2. Kayaking: Paddling along Croatia's coast is a peaceful way to discover hidden coves, sea caves, and calm inlets. The country's clear waters and varied shoreline provide kayaking opportunities for both beginners and experienced paddlers. Popular kayaking destinations include the Elafiti Islands, the Pakleni Islands, and the peaceful Mljet National Park.

3. Windsurfing and kiteboarding: Windsurfers and kiteboarders seeking thrilling rides on the waves flock to Croatia's windy spots, particularly around the islands of Bra, Korula, and the Peljeac Peninsula. These locations are ideal for high-energy water sports.

4. Sailing and yachting: Croatia's thousands of islands and islets make it a sailor's paradise. Explore the Adriatic's hidden treasures by chartering a yacht or joining a sailing tour. You can anchor in secluded bays, visit picturesque villages, and enjoy the allure of the sea at your own pace.

5. Cliff Diving: The dramatic cliffs along the Dalmatian coast provide an ideal setting for cliff diving. Popular locations such as the cliffs near Dubrovnik and the Blue Hole on Vis Island offer breathtaking leaps into the Adriatic's azure waters. It's an exciting way to see the coast from a different angle.

6. Cruises and Sea Tours: Cruises and sea tours are a relaxing way to discover the natural beauty of Croatia's coastline, archipelagos, and hidden treasures. Boat trips to the Blue Cave on Bievo Island or the Elafiti Islands near Dubrovnik provide glimpses of Croatia's stunning natural wonders.

7. Stand-Up Paddleboarding (SUP): Stand-up paddleboarding has grown in popularity along Croatia's coast. Rent a board and explore the calm bays, inlets, and clear waters at your leisure. SUP is a peaceful way to connect with the sea and enjoy breathtaking views.

8. Experiences with Fishing and Seafood: Fishing enthusiasts can join local fishermen on their daily outings or book a fishing excursion. It's an opportunity to try traditional fishing methods and enjoy the catch of the day. Seafood lovers can enjoy fresh and delicious dishes inspired by the Adriatic at local restaurants.

9. Swimming in Secret Coves: Discovering hidden coves and inlets perfect for swimming and sunbathing is one of the pleasures of the Croatian coast. Many of these hidden gems are only accessible by boat, ensuring a peaceful escape from the crowds.

Chapter 8: Food and Wine

Croatia's culinary scene is a delightful fusion of Mediterranean and Central European flavors, offering a diverse array of dishes that tantalize the taste buds. Seafood lovers can savor freshly caught Adriatic fish, while meat lovers can savor dishes like the renowned Croatian lamb or hearty stews. Pasticada, a slow-cooked beef dish, and truly, a delicious pastry filled with cheese, are two traditional specialties. The country's wine culture is equally impressive, with numerous vineyards producing high-quality wines such as Plavac Mali and Malvasia. Whether dining in coastal restaurants or family-owned konobas, Croatia's food and wine culture is a culinary journey to remember.

Croatian Cuisine

Croatian cuisine reflects the country's diverse landscapes, from the lush coastal regions to the hearty dishes of the interior. It's a unique culinary tapestry that combines Mediterranean and Central European influences.

1. Seafood Delights: Given Croatia's extensive coastline, seafood is a mainstay of Croatian cuisine. Fresh Adriatic

fish, such as sea bass, bream, and sardines, are prepared in a variety of ways, from grilled to baked with Mediterranean herbs. Scampi and mussels are also popular seafood options. Coastal towns like Dubrovnik and Split serve seafood in a variety of delectable dishes.

2. Roast Meats and Peke: Roasts and meat dishes reign supreme in Croatia's interior regions. Peka, a method of cooking under a bell-shaped lid, is used to prepare succulent lamb, veal, or octopus, as well as potatoes and vegetables. Evapi, small grilled sausages, are a popular street food, often served with ajvar, a red pepper condiment, and fresh bread.

3. Traditional Stews: Croatia has hearty stews that are ideal for savoring during the winter months. Pasticada, a slow-cooked beef dish marinated in wine and spices and served with gnocchi or pasta, is one of the most well-known. Gula, or goulash, is another popular comfort food.

4. Pasta and Risotto: Croatian pasta dishes include the iconic Trulli, a pastry filled with cottage cheese and sour cream that is often served as both a savory and sweet treat. Coastal regions are known for their seafood risottos, and Istria is known for its truffle-infused pasta dishes.

5. Fresh and local ingredients: Croatian cuisine emphasizes fresh, locally sourced ingredients. Many dishes include olive oil, herbs, and seasonal vegetables like tomatoes and zucchini. Even Croatian wine and cheese are popular due to their distinct regional flavors.

6. Baking Traditions: Croatian baking traditions are deeply rooted, offering a wide range of sweet and savory pastries. Traditional bread is a staple, and the coastal regions produce delectable breads such as black squid ink bread. During festive occasions, desserts such as Ukraine (doughnuts), frustule (small doughnuts), and pachinko (crepes) are consumed.

7. Local Flavors and Wine: Croatia is known for its distinct wine regions, each with its grape varieties and winemaking techniques. Plavac Mali, Malvasia, and Grapevine are some of the country's notable wine varieties. Olive oil is another prized product, with different regions producing their distinct flavors.

Wine and Culinary Tours

Croatia's burgeoning wine and culinary scene has become a magnet for food and wine enthusiasts looking for unique and authentic experiences. Wine and culinary tours in this Mediterranean jewel take you on a sensory journey through the country's rich history, diverse landscapes, and vibrant flavors.

Wine Tours:

Croatia's wine regions, which are scattered along its coast and inland, offer a diverse and exciting range of wines. Wine tours allow visitors to explore these regions, learn about local winemaking traditions, and sample a variety of vintages. Consider the following wine regions:

Istria: Known for its Malvasia and Teran wines, Istria's rolling hills and picturesque vineyards provide an idyllic backdrop for wine tours. Visit wineries in charming towns like Motovun and Gronjan.

Dalmatia: This region is home to the famous Plavac Mali grape, which produces robust red wines. The Peljeac Peninsula is a must-see, as are the vineyards on the islands of Bra and Hvar.

Korula: This Adriatic island is known for its Poip and Grk white wines. Visit the island's vineyards and family-owned wineries.

Slavonia: The Slavonia region of Croatia's interior is famous for its Graevina (Welschriesling). Explore its vineyards and sample this refreshing white wine.

Culinary Tours:

Croatian culinary tours allow visitors to delve into the country's diverse culinary traditions, which blend Mediterranean and continental influences. Here's what you can expect on these flavorful journeys:

Seafood Delights: Along the coast, you can savor the freshest seafood, from grilled fish to calamari. Culinary tours include visits to bustling fish markets and dinners in seaside restaurants featuring dishes such as black risotto and octopus salad.

Truffle Hunting in Istria: The Istrian peninsula is famous for its truffles. Take part in truffle hunting excursions with trained dogs and dine on truffle-infused dishes at local restaurants.

Traditional Dalmatian Dishes: Learn how to make traditional Dalmatian dishes like paticada, a slow-cooked beef stew, and the iconic peak dishes cooked under a bell-shaped lid.

Olive Oil and Cheese Tastings: Learn about the secrets of Croatian olive oil and cheese production. Enjoy tastings at local olive groves and family-run cheese farms.

Cooking Classes: Enroll in cooking classes to learn how to prepare Croatian specialties like pasticada, trukli, and more. Local chefs share their knowledge and culinary traditions.

The Experiment:

Wine and culinary tours in Croatia provide a complete experience. You not only savor exquisite food and wine, but you also meet local producers and chefs who are passionate about their craft. Exploring picturesque vineyards and savoring meals in charming coastal villages are integral parts of these tours, making them a delightful blend of culture, history, and gastronomy.

Local Food Markets

Local food markets in Croatia are thriving hubs of culinary activity, bringing together the country's rich agricultural traditions and coastal bounty. These markets provide an authentic and sensory experience, allowing you to immerse yourself in Croatia's flavors, scents, and culture.

1. Dolac Market in Zagreb: Dolac Market, also known as the "Belly of Zagreb," is one of the capital city's most famous markets. It is a bustling hub of fresh produce, flowers, and regional specialties located above the main square. Stalls are brimming with seasonal fruits and vegetables, and vendors sell cheeses, cured meats, and baked goods. The colorful umbrellas that shade the market create a lively atmosphere.

2. Split Green Market, Split: Split's Green Market, or "Pazar" as the locals call it, is a daily culinary spectacle. It's a fresh Mediterranean produce paradise located within Diocletian's Palace. Tomatoes, olives, figs, and citrus fruits are on display, along with locally caught seafood. You'll also find a delicious selection of dried herbs, spices, and local cheeses.

3. Rijeka Market, Rijeka: Rijeka's bustling market, also known as Placa, is a culinary treasure trove. It offers a wide variety of fresh seafood, including mussels and squid, as well as local fruits and vegetables and a selection of Istrian truffles and olive oils. The market reflects Rijeka's maritime heritage and coastal cuisine.

4. Katel Stari Fish Market, Katela: Croatia's fish markets are an essential part of the country's culinary scene. The Katel Stari Fish Market, located in a charming coastal town, allows you to see the daily catch brought in by local fishermen. It's an opportunity to buy fresh Adriatic fish and seafood, ideal for a seaside barbecue.

5. Farmers' Markets in Istria: Istria is well-known for its truffles, olive oil, and wine. Farmers' markets in the region, such as the one in Pula, have a wonderful selection of these products. Taste truffle-infused cheeses, local wines, and aromatic olive oils. The Istrian peninsula's rich gastronomy is on full display.

6. Ibenik Market, Ibenik: This bustling market near Ibenik's old town is a vibrant showcase of Dalmatian produce. Local fruit, vegetables, and aromatic herbs abound. The market is more than just a place to buy ingredients; it is also a cultural experience that showcases the essence of Dalmatian cuisine.

7. Zadar Market, Zadar: Zadar's market has an excellent selection of local delicacies such as dried figs, Pag cheese, and Maraschino cherries. This market is ideal for picking up unique food souvenirs to take home, allowing you to savor the flavors of Croatia long after your visit.

8. Local Fish Markets in Coastal Towns: Local fish markets can be found along the Croatian coast in picturesque towns such as Rovinj, Dubrovnik, and Makarska. These markets are the beating heart of seafood gastronomy. You can choose from a variety of fresh catch from the Adriatic and have it prepared at nearby restaurants.

Chapter 9: Practical Information

Croatian travelers should be aware of the currency (Croatian Kuna), the standard European plug type (Europlug), and the official language (Croatian). Croatia is in the Central European Time Zone (CET) and has a 230V/50Hz electrical system. When it comes to transportation, the extensive bus and ferry networks make getting around simple. Tourists should have travel insurance and, depending on their nationality, the appropriate visas. For a smooth and enjoyable stay in Croatia, dial 112 for emergency services. It is also advisable to have a basic understanding of local customs and tipping practices.

Transportation and Getting Around

Croatia's stunning landscapes, from coastal gems to historical towns and inland wonders, are best explored with a dependable and efficient transportation system. Here's a comprehensive guide to getting around and making the most of your visit to this Mediterranean jewel.

1. A Well-Connected Road Network: Croatia has an extensive road network, making it accessible by car from

neighboring European countries. Highways are well-maintained, and driving in Croatia is simple. The picturesque coastal highway known as the Jadranska Magistrala provides breathtaking views of the Adriatic.

2. Traveling by bus: Buses are a convenient and cost-effective way to travel within Croatia. The country has an extensive bus network that connects major cities, towns, and even remote villages. Many bus routes provide comfortable, air-conditioned coaches.

3. Trains: While Croatia's train network connects various regions, it is not as fast or as extensive as the bus network. Train travel can be scenic, especially on routes like Zagreb to Split, which pass through beautiful landscapes.

4. Ferries and island hopping: Ferries and catamarans are necessary for exploring Croatia's coastal islands. Numerous ferry routes connect the country's island-dotted coastline. Split, Dubrovnik, and Zadar are popular departure points for island hopping.

5. Renting a Car: Renting a car is an excellent option for travelers who want to explore remote areas and villages. If your license does not contain the Latin alphabet, you must have an International Driving Permit. Drive carefully and obey all local traffic laws.

6. Flights: Major cities such as Zagreb, Split, and Dubrovnik all have international airports, making air travel a convenient way to get into Croatia. Domestic flights connect various regions.

7. Local transportation: Trams and buses are common modes of local transportation within cities. The tram system in Zagreb is efficient, whereas coastal cities like Split and Dubrovnik rely on buses to connect neighborhoods.

8. Taxi Services: Taxis are readily available in most cities and towns. To avoid surprises, use a licensed taxi service with clear pricing. Uber is also available in some Croatian cities.

9. Cycling: Croatia's stunning landscapes make it an ideal destination for cyclists. You can explore coastal paths, mountain trails, and scenic routes. Bicycle rentals are available in tourist areas.

10. Travel Cards and Passes: Consider using travel cards or passes for city travel, which offer convenience and savings. For example, the Zagreb Card provides access to public transportation as well as discounts at various attractions.

11. Navigating Islands: When visiting the Croatian islands, consider purchasing island hopping passes, which provide flexibility for multiple ferry rides.

Accommodation Options

Croatia, with its captivating landscapes and rich history, offers a diverse range of accommodation options to suit all types of travelers. From historic coastal cities to charming villages and remote islands, here's a guide to finding the ideal place to stay during your visit to this Mediterranean gem.

1. Hotels and Resorts: Croatia's hotels and resorts offer a unique blend of comfort and luxury. Coastal cities like Dubrovnik, Split, and Rovinj have a wide range of high-end options. Many hotels have stunning sea views, spas, and excellent dining. Inland destinations such as Zagreb also have boutique and luxury accommodations.

2. Boutique Hotels: Boutique hotels in Croatia exude character and charm. They are frequently housed in historic structures and provide one-of-a-kind and personalized experiences. These accommodations allow you to immerse yourself in the rich history of the country.

3. Apartments and villas: Consider renting a villa or an apartment for a more independent and private stay. There are a variety of holiday homes available along the coast and on the islands, some with private pools and waterfront access. These are ideal for families or groups.

4. Pensions and guesthouses: Pensions and guesthouses offer travelers a cozy and cost-effective option. These can be found in a variety of cities and towns, providing comfortable stays with a personal touch.

5. Hostels: Croatia's hostels cater to budget-conscious travelers. They are commonly found in cities and popular tourist destinations and offer both dormitory-style and private room options. They're great for socializing and meeting other travelers.

6. Glamping and campsites: Croatia's natural beauty provides an ideal setting for camping and glamping. Campgrounds are plentiful, especially along the coast. You can also go "glamorous camping" in well-appointed tents or cabins with modern amenities.

7. Agritourism: Agritourism in rural and inland areas provides a unique opportunity to stay on working farms and vineyards. This immersive experience allows you to sample local cuisine and relax in the countryside.

8. Lighthouses: Croatia's coastline is dotted with historic lighthouses that now serve as unique accommodations. They provide a one-of-a-kind experience, often with dramatic sea views and a sense of isolation.

9. Boat and Yacht Stays: Consider staying on a boat or yacht in the coastal towns and islands. This maritime experience allows you to fall asleep to the gentle sounds of the Adriatic and enjoy a lifestyle synonymous with the Croatian coast.

10. Historic Accommodations: Croatia's historic cities have accommodations within ancient city walls or historical buildings, allowing you to relive the country's storied past. Staying within Dubrovnik's city walls or Diocletian's Palace in Split is an unforgettable experience.

11. Luxury Villas: Consider renting a luxury villa for opulence and privacy. Croatia has a plethora of luxurious properties with stunning architecture, private pools, and breathtaking views.

12. Stays Off the Beaten Path: Remote guesthouses or huts in Croatia's countryside or on its islands offer seclusion and an escape from the daily grind for those looking for remote and tranquil experiences.

Safety and Health Tips

Croatia is a relatively safe and welcoming country for visitors, but it is critical to prioritize your safety and well-being during your visit. Here are some safety and health tips to ensure a safe and enjoyable journey:

1. Travel Insurance:
Before your trip, purchase comprehensive travel insurance that covers medical emergencies, trip cancellations, and unexpected events. This is especially important when traveling abroad.

2. Health Preparations:
Check that your routine vaccinations are up to date. Consider vaccines for hepatitis A and B, rabies, and tick-borne encephalitis based on your travel plans and medical history. Consult your healthcare provider well in advance of your trip.

3. Sun protection:
Croatia's sunny climate means plenty of sun exposure. To avoid sunburn, bring sunscreen with a high SPF, sunglasses, a wide-brimmed hat, and lightweight clothing.

4. Hydration:

It is critical to stay hydrated, especially during the hot summer months. Carry a reusable water bottle and refill it regularly water is safe to drink, but bottled water is widely available.

5. Insect Protection:

When visiting wooded or rural areas, use insect repellent to protect yourself from ticks and mosquitoes, which can transmit diseases like Lyme disease and West Nile virus.

6. Food and water should be handled with caution:

Croatia has a safe and well-regulated food and water supply. Nonetheless, it is best to avoid street food vendors in busy tourist areas. To reduce the risk of foodborne illnesses, drink bottled water and eat at reputable restaurants.

7. Emergency Services:

In Croatia, dial 112. It is used for medical emergencies, fire, and police services. Keep this number in your phone and know how to contact the nearest embassy or consulate if you run into any legal or safety issues.

8. Local Laws and Customs:

Respect local laws and customs. Avoid public intoxication and disruptive behavior, especially in historic towns and city centers. When entering religious sites, some areas have strict dress codes.

9. Beach Safety:
Be aware of strong currents and changing weather conditions when swimming in the Adriatic. Follow lifeguard instructions and swim only in designated areas. If you intend to engage in water activities, bring the necessary beach and water safety equipment.

10. Currency and valuables:
To keep your valuables safe, use hotel safes or hidden money belts. While Croatia is generally safe, petty theft can occur in crowded tourist areas.

Useful Phrases and Tips

When traveling in Croatia, learning a few basic Croatian phrases will help you navigate the country and connect with locals. While many Croatians in tourist areas speak English, making an effort to speak the local language can enhance your experience. Here are some key phrases and tips to make your trip to Croatia more enjoyable:

1. Greetings:

- Hello: Bok (informal) / Dobar dan (formal)
- Good morning: Dobro jutro
- Good evening: Dobra Veer
- Goodbye, Dovienja
- Please: Molim
- Thank you very much:
- Yes: Da
- No: Ne

2. Basic Phrases:

- Excuse me: Oprostite
- I'm sorry: ao mi je
- I don't understand: Ne razumijem
- How much does this cost? Koliko to Kota
- Where is Kota Kotaoom? Where is the nearest WC?
- I need assistance: Trebam Pomo
- My name is [Your Name]: Zovem se [Your Name]
- Could you please assist me? Can you help me?
- Do you speak English? Do you speak English?

3. Dining and Food:

- Stol za: [number]

- I'd like to order: elim Maruti
- Water: Voda
- Menu: Meni
- Please bring the bill: Raun, mom
- Coffee: Kava
- Beer: Pivo
- Wine: Vino

4. Transportation:

- Where is the bus/train station? Where is the bus stop/station?
- How much is a plane ticket to [destination]? Do you have a car for [destination]?
- Taxi: Taxi
- Where is the airport? Where can I find Zrana Luka?
- How far is it to [destination]? Who is going to [destination]?

5. Shopping:

- How much is this? Koliko ovo kota?
- Can I pay with a credit card? Can you use a credit card?
- I'm just looking: Samo Razgledavam

- Is this available in a different color/size? Is ovo u drugoj boji/veliini?

6. Tipping:

- Tipping is customary in Croatia. In restaurants, cafes, and faxi servicfaxit is customary to leave a tip of 10-15%.

7. Local Etiquette:

- Croatians typically greet with a handshake and maintain eye contact throughout conversations. It is considered polite to address people with their (Mr., Mrs.) and last names.

8. Currency:

- Croatia uses the Croatian Kuna (HRK) as its currency. Understand exchange rates and keep a small amount of local currency on hand for smaller purchases.

9. Emergency Services:

- In Croatia, the emergency number is 112, which covers medical, fire, and police services.

Packing List

Packing for a trip to Croatia requires striking a balance between coastal, historical, and natural adventures. Here's a comprehensive packing list to ensure you're well-prepared for your Croatian adventure:

1. Travel Documents:

- PA passport and a photocopy
- Visa (if required)
- Details on travel insurance
- Confirmation of flights and lodging
- Driver's license (if renting a car)
- Contact information in the event of an emergency

2. Clothing:

- Summer clothing that is light and breathable, such as shorts, T-shirts, and swimwear.
- Comfortable walking shoes that are suitable for both city exploration and hiking.
- Dressier shoes for evenings out.
- A light jacket or sweater for cooler evenings, especially if visiting during the shoulder season.
- For unexpected showers, bring a rain jacket or umbrella.

- Sunglasses and a hat for protection.

3. Toiletries:

- Sunscreen with a high SPF.
- Insect repellent.
- Items of personal hygiene.
- Travel-sized first-aid kit.
- Medications (both prescription and over-the-counter).
- Toiletry bag containing the necessities.

4. Electronics:

- Universal plug adapter for European outlets.
- Smartphone and charger.
- Camera or GoPro for capturing the breathtaking scenery.
- Power bank for charging devices on the go.

5. Miscellaneous:

- Money belt or neck pouch for storing valuables.
- Daypack or travel backpack for daily excursions.
- Bottle of water that can be reused.
- Maps or a travel guidebook.
- Ziplock bags are great for keeping documents and electronics dry.

- Travel pillow and eye mask for restful sleep on long journeys.

6. Beach Essentials:

- Beach towel or sarong.
- Beach bag.
- If you intend to go snorkeling, bring your snorkeling equipment.
- Water shoes for rocky beaches.
- PWatertight phone pouch

7. Entertainment:

- A good book or e-reader.
- Downtime can be spent playing cards or traveling games.

8. Travel Accessories:

- Travel-sized laundry detergent for handwashing clothes.
- Luggage locks for added security.
- Sewing kit in travel size.
- Quick-drys travel towel for beach days or emergency use.
- Earplugs and a sleep mask for a good night's sleep.

9. Useful Items

- Lightweight day rain bag for carrying your essentials.
- Portable luggage scale to avoid excess baggage fees.
- Refillable water bottles help to reduce plastic waste.

10. Snacks:

- Non-perishable snacks for long journeys or when dining options are limited.

11. Outdoor Gear (if applicable):

- Hiking shoes and equipment if you intend to visit national parks.
- If you intend to camp, bring your camping gear.

Keep in mind that specific packing requirements may vary depending on the time of year and the activities you intend to participate in. It's always a good idea to check the weather forecast and research any special events or dress codes in the areas you'll be visiting. By being prepared, you can make the most of your trip and enjoy the diverse landscapes and experiences that Croatia has to offer.

Itinerary Plan

Croatia offers a wide range of experiences, from historic city explorations to idyllic coastal getaways and outdoor adventures. The ideal itinerary plan will be determined by your interests, the length of your stay, and the regions you wish to visit. Here are a few itinerary suggestions to help you make the most of your trip to Croatia:

1. The Coastal Splendor: Dubrovnik to Split (7-10 Days)

Day 1–3: Dubrovnik

- Explore the historic walled city of Dubrovnik.
- Explore the ancient city walls and the famous Fort Lovrijenac.
- Take a cable car ride for panoramic views.
- Relax on Banje Beach.

Day 4-5: Korula

- Ferry to the island of Korula.

- Explore the charming old town.
- Visit the birthplace of Marco Polo.
- Enjoy the island's pristine beaches.

Day 6-7: Hvar

- Sail to Hvar, known for its vibrant nightlife and beautiful beaches.
- Discover the historic sites of Hvar Town.
- Visit the stunning Pakleni Islands.
- Experience Hvar's famous nightlife.

Day 8-10: Split

- Visit the historic city of Split.
- Discover Diocletian's Palace and its numerous museums.
- Hike to Marjan Hill for panoramic views.
- Take a day trip to the enchanting Plitvice Lakes National Park.

2. Historical and Cultural Exploration: Zagreb to Plitvice to Zadar (7 Days)

Day 1-3: Zagreb

- Begin in Zagreb, the capital.
- Explore the Upper and Lower Towns.

- Visit St. Mark's Church and the Museum of Broken Relationships.
- At local restaurants, savor Croatian cuisine.

Day 4-5: Plitvice Lakes National Park

- Visit Plitvice Lakes National Park.
- Hike through lush forests and see stunning waterfalls.
- Explore the park's upper and lower lakes.
- Stay overnight in the park or nearby.

Day 6-7: Zadar

- Visit Zadar, a historic coastal city.
- Admire the Sea Organ and Greeting to the Sun installations.
- Explore Zadar's old town and Roman ruins.
- Relax on Zadar's beautiful beaches.

3. Island-Hopping Adventure: Split to Dubrovnik via the Islands (10 Days)

Day 1-3:

- Begin in Split and explore the historic center.
- Visit Diocletian's Palace and the local markets.

- Take a boat to the nearby island of Bra for a day trip.

Day 4-5: Hvar

- Sail to Hvar, which is known for its vibrant nightlife.
- Explore Hvar Town and the nearby beaches.
- Enjoy the beauty of the Pakleni Islands.

Day 6-7: Vis

- Travel to the remote island of Vis.
- Visit Vis and the famous Blue Cave Rilievo.
- At family-owned konobas, you can savor regional cuisine.

Day 8-10: Dubrovnik

- Travel to Dubrovnik via the lovely island of Korula.
- Explore Dubrovnik's historic center and city walls.
- Take a cable car ride for panoramic views.
- Relax on the beaches and explore the nearby Elafiti Islands.

These are just a few suggestions for planning the ideal Croatia itinerary. You can tailor your itinerary to your interests, whether they are history and culture, coastal relaxation, or outdoor adventures. Croatia's diverse landscapes and rich heritage provide countless opportunities for a memorable journey.

Frequently Asked Questions

- Do I need a visa to visit Croatia?

Most tourists from the EU and the US can enter Croatia without a visa for up to 90 days.

- What is the currency in Croatia?

Croatia uses the Croatian Kuna (HRK) as its currency.

- Is it safe to travel in Croatia?

Croatia is generally safe for tourists, with low crime rates.

- When is the best time to visit Croatia?

Warm weather is best from May to September, but it can be crowded during the peak summer season.

- Are credit cards widely accepted in Croatia?

Yes, credit cards are widely accepted, particularly in tourist areas.

- Is it safe to drink the water in Croatia?

Most of Croatia's tap water is safe to drink.

- Do people in Croatia speak English?

Yes, English is widely spoken, particularly in tourist areas.

- How can I get around Croatia?

Buses, ferries, trains, and car rentals are all viable modes of transportation.

- Can I use Euros in Croatia?

While some establishments may accept Euros, it is preferable to use the local currency, Kuna.

- Is there a dress code for churches and religious sites?

When visiting religious sites, modest clothing is advised; shoulders and knees should be covered.

- What are some traditional Croatian dishes to try?

Try Peka, evapi, and pasticada. Seafood is also a must-try along the coast.

- Are there many vegetarian or vegan options in Croatia?

Vegetarian and vegan options are available, but they are less common in traditional cuisine.

- What is the tipping custom in Croatia?

Tipping is appreciated; 10-15% is customary in restaurants.

- Can I use my cellphone in Croatia?

Yes, most international mobile networks operate in Croatia.

- Is there anything I should know about customs or etiquette?

Greet with a handshake, use polite language, and address people by their titles (Mr., Mrs.) and last names.

- Is it easy to find Wi-Fi in Croatia?

Wi-Fi is widely available in cafes, restaurants, and hotels.

- What are some must-see national parks in Croatia?

Plitvice Lakes, Krka, and Paklenica National Parks are popular choices.

- Is Croatia a family-friendly destination?

Croatia is a family-friendly destination, with numerous activities for children and family-friendly accommodations.

- Is there an ATM in Croatia?

Yes, ATMs are widely available in cities and tourist areas.

- Can I visit Croatian islands and how do I get there?

Yes, you can visit Croatian islands by taking ferries or catamarans from the mainland. Popular islands include Hvar, Bra, and Korula.

Conclusion

The recently published Croatia Travel Guide for 2024 is a comprehensive and up-to-date resource designed to help travelers explore Croatia's enchanting beauty and rich culture. This guide is a traveler's best friend, providing detailed information on every aspect of a Croatian trip.

The guide begins with an irresistible introduction that captivates readers, setting the stage for an unforgettable adventure in Croatia. It then delves into a well-organized 9-chapter table of contents, with each chapter thoughtfully crafted to cater to a variety of interests and preferences. This guide covers everything from exploring different regions of Croatia to delving into its history, culture, and culinary delights.

The meticulously crafted itineraries provide travelers with options for making the most of their visit, whether they seek coastal bliss, historical immersion, or outdoor adventures. Practical information and health and safety tips ensure that travelers are well-prepared for their trip, and useful phrases and frequently asked questions make navigating Croatia a breeze.

This Croatia Travel Guide is more than just a book; it's a portal to an unforgettable experience. It captures the essence of this Mediterranean gem, and with its wealth of information, vivid descriptions, and helpful tips, it equips travelers to create their own Croatian story, full of memories that will last a lifetime. Whether you're a first-time visitor or a seasoned traveler, the Croatia Travel Guide 2024 is a must-have companion for your Croatian adventure.

Printed in Great Britain
by Amazon

36480193R00062